Mary Anne Thompson
with the regards of
H. C.

MEMOIR

OF

JOHN BARSTOW.

A

BRIEF MEMOIR

OF

JOHN BARSTOW,

OF

PROVIDENCE, R. I.

BY

ALEXIS CASWELL.

[REPRINTED FROM THE NEW ENGLAND HISTORICAL AND GENEALOGICAL REGISTER, FOR OCTOBER, 1864.]

ALBANY, N. Y.:
PRINTED BY J. MUNSELL,
FOR PRIVATE DISTRIBUTION.
1864.

MEMOIR

OF

JOHN BARSTOW.

It is the dictate of wisdom, no less than the impulse of friendship, to perpetuate the memory of an honorable and useful life. It is for these reasons that the following brief memoir has been prepared.

John Barstow was born in Scituate, (now South Scituate,) Mass., on the 11th of February, 1791. He was the oldest son of John Burden Barstow, of Scituate, and Betsey Eells, of Hanover, Mass. He was a descendant of the sixth generation from William Barstow, who, with his brother George, left England in 1635 and came to this country in the ship Truelove. William, as appears from the public records of Dedham, Mass., was a resident in that town, in 1636. It is probable that he soon removed to Scituate where his descendants have continued to reside to the present time. The parents of the subject of this memoir, while he was but an infant, bought an estate in the town of Hanover, known as the "Broad Oak," where they built a spacious and, for those times, a very handsome and sightly house, which has continued to be the family residence for nearly three-quarters of a century. They were both of them persons of large capacities for business, of great energy of character, and of untiring industry; and, of course, were always "well to do in the world." The father, Colonel Barstow, (by which title he was generally known,) following the example of two or three of his immediate ancestors, for many years carried on the business of shipbuilding in connection with the cultivation of the soil. He long held a prominent place among the citizens of his town and county. His house was always open and noted for its hospitality. It was often the resort of men in the pursuit of business and participated largely in the social intercourse of the place. It was here, under the fostering care of the best of mothers that the son spent all the earlier years of his youth. He watched the progress of shipbuilding from the laying of the keel to the bolting on of the last plank and the rigging of the last sail; he listened to the conversation and narratives of shipmasters and voyagers ; he gathered up unheeded many items of information respecting commerce and trade, the perils and successes of a seafaring life; he looked out almost daily upon the ocean and was familiar with its calms and storms. It is not easy to say how much the early bent of his mind and the predilections of his later life were determined by these circumstances. They evidently were not without a marked influence.

Of the occupations of his youth he himself has said that his "time was divided between farming, study and teaching until the twentieth year of his age." His first preceptress was Miss Priscilla Mann, who taught the town school at "Broad Oak," and who, as another pupil of hers remarks, "for more than half a century had been distinguished in that capacity." He has been heard to refer to her with great respect except that she once punished him without just cause. I mention this to show how early he was accustomed to govern himself and judge others by the principle of justice. After enjoying the benefit of such schools as the vicinity afforded he was sent to the Academy in Fairhaven, then under the charge of a Mr. Gould. In the autumn of 1806, he was sent to the Academy at Sandwich and placed under the instruction of Mr. Elisha Clapp, who appears to have possessed eminent qualifications as a teacher, and who, during the period of his preceptorship, about twelve years, placed the Sandwich Academy among the best classical schools in the State. Mr. Clapp was a graduate of Harvard College, and had been a tutor there; and, from the testimony of more than one of his distinguished pupils must have carried with him to the Academy a rare ability and a genuine love for teaching.

Young Barstow entered the Academy with the intention of preparing for admission to Harvard College. He remained there probably about two years. Several of his fellow students with whom he formed lasting friendships, have risen to honorable distinction in professional and public life. He was in the same class with Peleg Sprague, the distinguished District Judge of the United States Court, in Massachusetts, and of Jonathan M. Wainwright, late Bishop of the Episcopal Church, in the State of New York. The Hon. Albert Smith and the Hon. Francis Bassett, both of Boston, were members of the Academy at the same time. Concerning his character as a student, I venture to offer the following testimony, extracted from a recent letter of a schoolmate, whose judgment is entitled to high respect. He says, "his character and habits were then as in after life:—the former being noted for the high qualities of truth, honor, and unswerving integrity, and the latter for gentlemanly bearing and circumspection under all circumstances. In these respects he was acknowledged to be one of the models of the school. As a student he was persistent, never succumbing to difficulties. He was particularly distinguished in the mathematics." And, from other testimonies I infer that he scarcely fell behind the foremost of his class in the Latin and Greek languages. From my own observation I can well credit the statements of his early proficiency in these studies. Through life he retained a far better knowledge of Latin and especially of geometry, algebra, and trigonometry than most students, whose after lives like his, were thoroughly engrossed with business. Ceaseless industry, and a determination to master whatever study he undertook marked his character as a student. With his high appreciation of scholarship, his love of study, and his aptitude in learning, a noble career was open before him. The best results of intellectual culture might well have been anticipated as the reward of his labor. But a sendentary life was found not to be conducive to his health, and in his twentieth year, as before stated, he turned his attention to more active pursuits. Brought up almost within sight of the ocean and familiar from his boyhood with ships and shipbuilding it was not unnatural that his predeliction should be for a seafaring life; and upon this he soon entered, commencing at the lowest round of the ladder and working his way up to the summit. In the progress of a few years he became the master and owner of several merchant vessels engaged chiefly in the European trade.

In the meantime his love of study did not forsake him, and his intercourse with the commercial business of foreign ports probably suggested to him the importance of being able to speak the French language, then, as now, the common language of Europe. Accordingly, in 1814, as nearly as I can determine, he repaired to Paris where he spent a year in perfecting himself in the French language and in pursuing at the Free College of France such other studies as were suited to his tastes and subservient to his progress in life. This was during the closing period of the reign of the Emperor Napoleon I. He often saw the great captain whom no one, it seems, ever saw without carrying away a deep impression of the dignity of his personal presence. He was in Paris during the eventful *Hundred Days*, in the spring of 1815, and was present when Napoleon reviewed his grand army,—the grandest, perhaps, which Europe had ever seen,—before leaving his capitol to measure himself with Wellington on the field of Waterloo. His studies at the College of France were turned to excellent account. Besides several branches of more general knowledge pursued, at the same time, he acquired such a ready use of the French language as to be of the greatest practical service to him on many occasions in after life.

Soon after his return from France, Mr. Barstow purchased a vessel and sailed for Stockholm, where he disposed of vessel and cargo and spent a large portion of the season in travels in the North of Sweden. After a second brief visit to Paris, he again returned home. Not long after this, probably in 1817, he formed a business connection with Mr. Jacob Barker, of New York, then extensively engaged in shipping, banking, and general business. During this connexion Mr. Barstow spent three years in New Orleans, devoted chiefly to the management of Mr. Barker's banking and commission business in that section of the country. It was also, I think, during this period that he spent a year in the West Indies and one in Bermuda. Circumstances, it is believed, not altogether agreeable to him, led him to close his business connection with Mr. Barker; and he again turned his attention to commerce. He was again for several years engaged in the European trade, sailing for the most part in vessels built for him in his native town.

During this whole period of Mr. Barstow's early career his

knowledge of business, and general character, were such as to command the confidence of the mercantile community wherever he was known. The war of 1812 had gone far to impoverish the country. Capital was scarce and difficult to be obtained, yet Mr. Barstow's credit was always sufficient to command all the capital which he deemed it wise to employ in his business. A gentleman of high standing as a merchant, and, at that time, member of a large commercial house in New York, says in a recent letter, speaking of Mr. Barstow: "I remember that such was the entire confidence of myself and partner in his integrity, ability and energy that we did not hesitate to advance him whatever capital he wanted for building or buying vessels." It is hardly necessary to add that during the ten or twelve years in which he was engaged in these various pursuits his success, if not equal to his wishes, was at least equal to all reasonable expectations; and placed him in a position to enter upon a wider field of business under the most favorable auspices.

On the first of January, 1828, he formed a copartnership with his friend and relative Caleb Barstow, of New York, and embarked in the general shipping and commission business under the firm of C. & J. Barstow. In the autumn of the same year he was married to Sarah Swoope, second daughter of Edward K. Thompson, of Providence, R. I.; and added the interesting and agreeable cares of the household to those of the counting room. In his new business connection opening as it did an extensive field of operations, he soon became prominent among his commercial associates. His knowledge of business on a broad scale, his sound judgment and his uniform courtesy made him welcome in every circle where the interests of trade were under consideration. A commercial friend speaking of him at that time says, "there was a high toned sense of honor about him and a dignified presence that commanded the respect of all with whom he had intercourse." He was soon elected a member of the Chamber of Commerce, and a Director in the Bank of America, one of the first banks in the city. He discharged the duties of both of these trusts with high credit, the former for several years, the latter until he left New York, in 1838. The firm of C. & J. Barstow was continued for ten years with gratifying success. They were largely interested in the first line of packets that sailed regularly between New York and New Orleans. The tastes of the partners determined their respective departments of business. The former took the supervision of the counting room and the sale of merchandise; the latter had charge of the shipping and of the outdoor business generally. It may be added that during the entire continuance of the firm the warmest friendship subsisted between the partners, and was severed only by the hand of death.

In the autumn of 1838, partly perhaps, from a desire to change his line of business and partly in deference to the known wishes of some of his friends, Mr. Barstow withdrew from the firm, closed his business connections in New York and removed to Providence, R. I. This removal involved not a cessation of activity, but only a new sphere of action. We shall merely glance at some of his more important business connections subsequent to this removal.

While engaged in his previous pursuits he had often occasion to cultivate his mechanical aptitudes. One of the marked elements of his mind was that of constructing and organizing. His long familiarity with the building, rigging, and sailing of ships had made him conversant with practical mechanics, as his early studies had taught him its scientific principles. Foreseeing the great and growing demand for steam power in our industrial progress, he soon connected himself with the manufactory of steam engines, then scarcely advanced beyond its infancy in any part of the country. He at first formed a connection and embarked in business under the firm of Clark, Fairbanks & Co., which after a few years, with some change of partners was merged in the firm of Corliss, Nightingale & Co. For reasons which no one knew so well as himself, his name did not appear in either of these firms. He preferred to give the prominency to others, while it is well known that his command of capital and his rare capacity for business were essential to their progress. Indeed, it is not too much to say that the eminent success of the very extensive establishment of Corliss, Nightingale & Co., second, as we presume, to no other of the kind in this country, was largely due to his financial ability and resources and his personal influence.

He was the second president of the Providence and Worcester Railroad, and during the completion of its construction and in the settlement of contested claims for land damages which were numerous and often difficult of adjustment, he rendered most important services to the corporation. He was for several years the efficient president of the Commercial Steamboat Company, which has done so much to facilitate the transmission of merchandise between the cities of Providence and New York. This agency, now seemingly indispensable to our commerce, and indeed, forming an era in its history, owes its success and present magnitude, to say the least, as much to him as to any other single man. Every day at a fixed hour the company despatched a capacious boat ladened with freight to New York, and every day, at almost as fixed an hour, another equally ladened arrived from thence. In the construction and equipment of the very considerable number of expensive boats necessary to the service, and in the general management of the business, the sound judgment and skill of the president were too conspicuous to be overlooked. The marked success of the company did not inure to the benefit of the stockholders alone, but to the commerce of the city as well. For nearly twenty-three years he was a director in the Boston and Providence Railroad. No office was with him a sinecure or a mere matter of form. If he accepted a position he took it with all its duties and responsibilities. As a director of the railroad he gave minute and personal attention to every question of importance which came up in the course of business. There was no negociation, no question of policy, no contract of any magnitude which did not pass under his examination; and few that were not benefitted by his suggestions. Outside of the official corps, who were wholly devoted to the business of the company, we think it quite safe to say that there was no one so thoroughly conversant as he, with its condition, its daily working and all its accounts. Of these services it is remarked, by a gentleman whose official position gives him a special right to speak, "he discharged every duty promptly and faithfully, and the corporation is under very deep obligations to him for the energy and sound judgment with which he, for so long a period promoted their interests." For thirteen years prior to his death he was the President of the Exchange Bank, one of the old and important banks of the city of his adoption.

These are some of the positions which he occupied with honor to himself and benefit to the public. In all of them he showed the same soundness of judgment, the same energy, the same dignity of character, the same high sense of just and honorable dealing. His business habits were exact, thorough and exhaustive. Whatever once passed his examination and approval was seldom altered by subsequent revision. He carried to every enterprise in which he was engaged such large and versatile capacity for business, and such untiring perseverance as to render success almost a matter of certainty. And it was seldom that, in this respect, he had any reason to be dissatisfied with the results of his labors.

Mr. Barstow was well informed on the history and political condition of the country, and especially upon its financial condition and industrial resources. He had, at the same time, a decided aversion to politics and would never consent to be a candidate for any political office. He seldom thought it worth while to discuss party questions with those whose opinions differed widely from his own. He belonged to the Republican party, was highly conservative, never extreme. He reverenced the constitution and held to the supremacy of law. He had a just abhorance of the institution of slavery. But until the breaking out of the present rebellion he held as most sensible persons did, that its management and the responsibility of its removal belonged to the states in which it was established. Yet he foresaw and deprecated its malignant and disturbing power upon the peace and harmony of the union. On the breaking out of the rebellion he felt himself called upon by every principle of patriotism and humanity to sustain the government. And though he knew the Southern character well and comprehended in a good degree the magnitude of the undertaking, he never entertained any doubts that the rebellion would, at length, be crushed and the supremacy of the constitution and the laws established in all the revolted states. Nor did he doubt that the institution of slavery would go down in the struggle never more to rise within the limits of the United States.

Through a long and busy life Mr. Barstow's fondness for books never forsook him. He was no reader of light literature, but found always a fresh interest in standard works on history, geography, scientific travels and explorations, and works on the industrial and commercial progress and resources of different nations. On all these topics he was well informed. He had found time, or made time for a large amount of reading and was gifted with a memory remarkably tenacious of whatever he had once known. He brought to the social intercourse of life such a storehouse of general knowledge as to make him always an interesting and instructive companion. Intellectual activity was the habit of his mind, and at the same time a source of real enjoyment. If a stormy day chanced to keep him at home he might be found with his table covered with books, settling for himself with the zeal of a professional student some disputed point of history, or chronology, or some mooted problem in mechanics, or navigation, or astronomy. Night might find him unwearied but not satisfied; and the inquiry would be sure to be resumed at his earliest leisure.

The publication of a large work on English Grammar some years since by his friend, Mr. Goold Brown, recalled his attention to that subject. Many were the evenings that he gave to the critical examination of the rules and principles, the grammatical forms and construction of the English language.

He was particularly interested in all the historical researches connected with the early settlers of New England. He, in some instances, instituted researches himself at home and abroad to elucidate that subject. He was a liberal patron of the Historic-Genealogical Society of New England, which has done so much to awaken an interest in our ancestral history. For several years prior to his death he was one of the vice-presidents of that society.

One trait of character as noble as it is rare he possessed in an unusual degree, and that was his active interest and sympathy in the success of meritorious young men commencing business under difficulties. He spontaneously advised with them, gave them the benefit of his own extended observation and experience; and what was more, he often added the rarer benefit of giving them credit and pecuniary aid till their business relations had become well established. Their success was to him a source of sincere pleasure. More than one under whose eyes this paragraph may fall will bear grateful testimony to the truth of these remarks.

Another trait of character equally worthy of notice will be recognized by all who knew him well. It was his unselfish readiness to serve his friends. It was never too early, never too late for them to call upon him. He was never too busy to give them an interview and do them any favor in his power. His own ease, or comfort, or indulgence never stood in the way of a kind act that could be of real use to a friend. Nor was his benevolence of this kind at all limited to those who might be entitled to claim the benefits of friendship. In every community there will be lone persons, widows, and orphans, who are left with a little property which is their sole dependence for support, and which they are totally incapable of managing to advantage. It was the fortune of my friend to be the counselor and helper of many such. He took the charge of their little business and advised them with as much care as if it had been a great business of his own. To one he recommended the savings bank, to another a life insurance, or a life annuity as the case might be; to a third some other investment. Nor did he stop with a mere recommendation, which would often, practically, be of no use. He saw that the investments were made and the legal papers carefully preserved. In several cases of this sort, from motives of pure kindness, he went so far, as to collect the annual dividends for a series of years, often at some little inconvenience, and pay them over to the owners.

In his own numerous circles of relatives there was scarcely one who was not the object of his care and many the recipients of most liberal aid. If any of them failed of the success they aimed at, it was not for the want of sound advise and generous assistance on his part.

Mr. Barstow was himself an accurate and expert accountant. He has been heard to say that if there was any one department of business in which he felt quite at home it was in bookkeeping and in the adjustment of complicated accounts. He often sat down to the examination of accounts of this description with all the zest that other men sit down to a game of chess. He was familiar with the different modes of bookkeeping in use among merchants. So important did he deem a knowledge of accounts, that he thought every young man, whatever his calling or purpose in life, should be taught the art of bookkeeping so far at least as to keep an accurate account of all his own pecuniary transactions. He held, and justly too, that it was an important element of success. Several of the youths of his family circle have received from him special and systematic instruction on this subject. The course would, perhaps, be closed by the presentation on his part of a set of books prepared for the use of his pupil.

I refer to these unostentatious modes of doing good, not for their individual importance but as indices of character. They ever point to one who finds a sincere pleasure in promoting the welfare of others.

In social intercourse, he retained in a great degree the characteristics of a refined gentleman of the old school. His manner was alwas friendly and courteous, but dignified, sometimes tending to the formal. He was generous in his hospitality, generous in the use of his property, and specially considerate of the poor and the unfortunate. Every object of public or private charity was sure of his support. The records of nearly all our benevolent institutions will bear ample testimony to his liberality. I refrain from mentioning several donations, made unsolicited within a year or two of his death, which do great credit to his generosity simply because it was not his wish that any special publicity should be given to them.

In conversation, the subject of this memoir was direct and explicit. His opinions, on most subjects, were well formed and definite; and when he had occasion to state them he did it clearly with the reasons and grounds upon which they rested. His manner was ordinarily quiet, but when he became earnest in discussion it was often animated and emphatic. His look, attitude and gesture added force to his arguments. He was always a most respectful and courteous listener to the opinions of others. It was apparently a fixed principle with him not to interrupt a person while speaking, but to listen silently to the end of his remarks. He was no teller of stories and had but moderate respect for persons who were occupied in that line of business. He sometimes referred to an illustrative anecdote, but always briefly. Jokes and puns sometimes provoked a smile, but they were not congenial to the bent of his mind. They subserved no purpose of life which had value in his estimation. His temperament was cheerful and hopeful. No difficulty brought despondence to his mind, no danger brought dismay. He worked on from morning till night as if there were no obstacles in his way, and then slept.

In stature he was of medium height, with full chest, compactly built; and, in his early life, as I judge, he had more than the ordinary share of muscular strength and physical endurance. He was uniformly an early riser. The morning hours were turned to valuable account not only in making his toilet, which was always done with scrupulous care, but in arranging for the business of the day.

My lamented friend was for many years an exemplary communicant in the Episcopal Church and one of its most liberal supporters. He made every preparation for his own departure with the utmost composure and serenity of mind. "The Lord is my shepherd, I shall not want," was his remark to a friend shortly before his death, and failing strength scarce permitted him to say more. After a somewhat protracted illness, from disease of the heart, he died peacefully in the bosom of his family, with his mental faculties unimpaired, in the assured hope of a better life beyond the grave. As a son, husband, and father, his life in every respect was most worthy of esteem and commendation. He left a wife and two daughters,—Lydia Kinnicutt and Elizabeth Thompson,—and a large circle of friends to cherish his memory, while mourning his loss.

Providence, August 24, 1864.

www.ingramcontent.com/pod-product-compliance
Lightning Source LLC
LaVergne TN
LVHW020638110826
845149LV00004B/1264

* 9 7 8 1 4 1 8 1 9 0 6 9 9 *